# Praise for
# *Baby Bandage and His First Aid Family*

"One of the most challenging things to do is break down medical concepts to toddlers and preschool children. Not only does Dr. Laurie accomplish this in *Baby Bandage*, but she makes it enjoyable and, consequently. retainable for children. A knowledgeable child is less fearful both in the office and at home and, armed with information, shows curiosity for future learning."

Zev Ash, MD, F.A.A.P., pediatrician

"Dr. Zelinger's work with children continues to be amazing. Our grandchildren love *Baby Bandage*, love wearing adhesive bandages and are now learning how medical materials are important and can be fun. I will certainly recommend this book to other families."

Lisa and Bob Topal

"*Baby Bandage* offers a gentle introduction to children about first aid and wound care. The illustrations are colorful, engaging and provide easy visualization and understanding for young readers. The Bandage Family' is relatable and is a pleasurable analogy to read!"

Courtney Juma, Certified Physician's Assistant (PA-C), urgent care center

"After reading Zelinger's delightful book *Baby Bandage*, I plan to carry it in my 'Granny' bag along with the other must-haves—toys, band aids, wipes and plenty of hugs. It is great to know that while we can't always protect our kids from every cut and scrape, we have the resourceful *Baby Bandage and His First Aid Family* to help us out. And what is better for healing than band aids and laughter!"

Lauren E. Persons, author of
*What Happened to Chester? An En-deer-ing Tale of Hope and Healing*

"As a child psychotherapist and Mom to an active preschool-age son, *Baby Bandage* is of great value to me! Being able to explain the natural process of bodily healing, along with the functional purpose of the many items we routinely stock our shelves with, is so helpful to our curious little ones. Another wonderful resource from Dr. Laurie Zelinger!"

Jillian Kelly-Wavering, LCSW, RPT-S, author of My *Grief Is Like the Ocean*

"Not only does *Baby Bandage* provide basic medical information to prepare young children for the inevitable 'booboos' while exploring their world, it has several other important messages within. Children will learn that everyone has a purpose no matter how small and their role in their family has meaning. I also love the diversity of the Bandage family and how important they are to each other. Dr. Zelinger provides a humorous story that children of all ages will find entertaining and meaningful."

Kim Larkins, LCSW, author of
*Practicing Mindfulness: Emma Lou the Yorkie Poo's Activity and Coloring Boo for Kids*

"Dr Zelinger's *Baby Bandage* is another must-have for parents, health professionals, educators and all who love or care for children. Her endearing characters, engaging and age-appropriate story and accompanying parent notes help alleviate the anxiety and fear often associated with childhood injuries, while reinforcing the family values of love, empathy and resiliency."

Darlene Glasser, RN, MSED, retired school nurse

"I absolutely loved *Baby Bandage*! Dr. Zelinger's characters and fun illustrations take the fear out of 'booboos' and all things associated with them. In addition, her skillful storytelling weaves in essential lessons on confidence, patience and recognizing the important roles we all play in this world. *Baby Bandage* is a wonderful resource for parents and educators alike."

Linda Abraham MLS, Peninsula Public Library

"Dr. Zelinger creates a make-believe world where first aid remedies are personified. Through story and illustration, children enter this world and discover that bandages come in all sizes, colors and shapes and have different and important roles. Young children love covering their 'ouchies,' and this story will hold their attention and teach them valuable lessons. As an early childhood educator and a grandma, I recommend *Baby Bandage* to encourage dialogue about little hurts and booboos."

Barbara Alster, MS, early childhood education teacher

# Baby Bandage and His First Aid Family:

## Healing Little Hurts and Booboos

# By Laurie Zelinger, PhD
## Illustrator Elisa Sabella

Loving Healing Press
Ann Arbor, MI

ISBN 978-1-61599-730-5 paperback
ISBN 978-1-61599-731-2 hardcover
ISBN 978-1-61599-732-9 eBook
Audiobooks available from Audible.com and iTunes

Published by
Loving Healing Press
5145 Pontiac Trail
Ann Arbor, MI 48105

www.LHPress.com
info@LHPress.com

Tollfree 888-761-6268 (USA/CAN/PR)
FAX 734-663-6861

Distributed by
Ingram (USA/CAN/AU), Betram's Books (UK/EU)

LOVING
HEALING
PRESS

# Contents

# Introduction

*Inspired by my grandchildren and dedicated to *every* body

The story of *Baby Bandage and His First Aid Family: Healing Little Hurts and Booboos* evolved after a day spent with my young grandchildren. When one of them needed to cover a small cut on his finger, I reached into my handbag and took out the only adhesive bandage I faithfully carried with me – a full size, sticky protector. My skeptical 4-year-old grandson watched with scrutiny as I wound it around and around his small finger with promises that we could replace it with a smaller one when we got home. That night, he asked for a bedtime story, and so, this story was born.

While an entertaining story for young children, this book also offers several messages. It provides basic information about first aid, it helps children identify with the difficult concept of having to wait for something they want, it reassures children that they can manage short separations from their family and it assists with building self-esteem. Children are reminded that even though they are small, they are important, and they can be given a job that helps others.

I hope that the young child sitting with you enjoys the story and that the book provides a chuckle for the adults reading it to them. Cuddling encouraged.

Dr. Laurie Zelinger, child psychologist
aka "Bubbe" (*grandmother*)

Once upon a time, there was a family of adhesive bandage strips that had a mother, father and three children. They shared a family resemblance, because they all had sticky legs and a soft, white, cotton rectangular patch on their belly.

Papa Bandage and Mama Bandage were the biggest, brother Bobby and sister Bella Bandage were middle sized kids and Baby Bandage was the littlest. They all lived together in a cozy cardboard box on a shelf in the back of a store. A sign saying *First Aid* hung above them.

The Bandage family lived above their cousins, Elastic Bandage, who they called "Stretch" for short, Gauze Bandage, Sterile Gloves and Cotton Balls, who were always bouncing around and making the shelf jiggle. And right next to them were Uncle Al – Al Cohol, that is – and Grandma Betty Dine, who was a special soap known all over the world for being excellent at cleaning cuts.

Their distant relatives, way down at the other end of the shelf, were the Tweezers, the Adhesive Tapes and the Ice Pack families, but their kids preferred to be called by their nicknames: Tweezy Wheezy, Sticky and Cool Aide.

Grandma Betty Dine had twin girls, Auntie and Septic, who were exactly alike, but since people couldn't tell them apart, they just combined their names and called them Antiseptic. Betty Dine took her twins everywhere she went, because they were the perfect cream for killing germs after she cleaned the skin, even though they might sting a teensy bit. But that was just for a little while. Sometimes, Uncle Al went along with them, too.

Whenever Grandma Betty and her cleanup crew finished taking care of a cut, scrape, splinter or blister, they would call one of their Bandage relatives to come and cover it up. That's what bandages are for. They don't fix stomach aches, sore throats or ear infections. But they do protect booboos from germs after you wash and pat your skin dry. And they let a scab grow underneath if your body is going to make one.

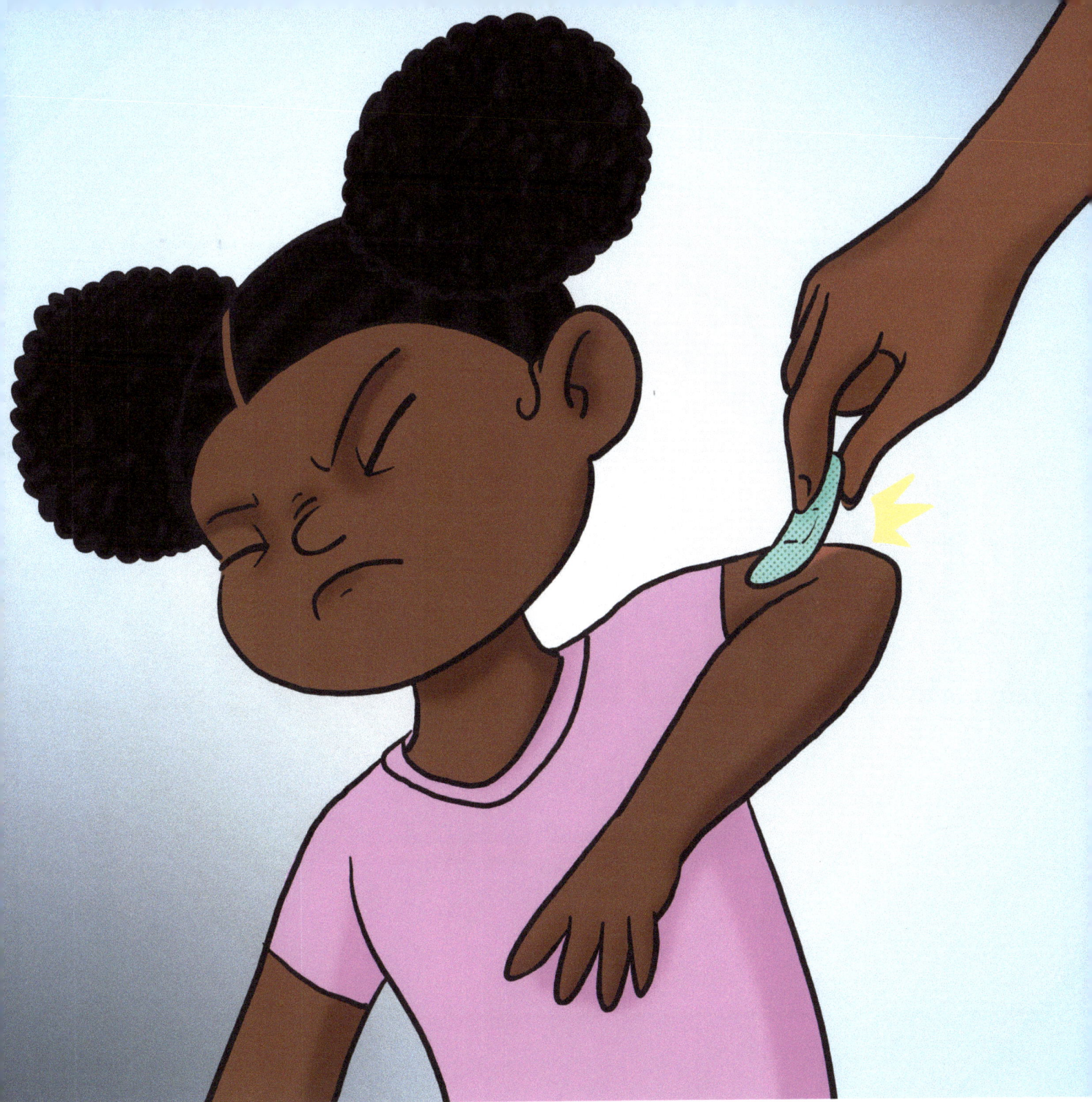

Bandages prevent you from scratching the sore area if it feels itchy while it heals. They don't hurt one little bit when they are on, but sometimes they ouch a little when you take them off.

Baby was so proud of his relatives. He had cousins, aunts and uncles that came in different colors and sizes and shapes. The fancy ones even had cool pictures on their backs. Whenever they got all mixed together in someone's drawer, they looked like a colorful parade.

Baby Bandage thought that living in a store was kind of nice. There were visitors all day long, but it was nice and quiet at night. Every day, people would come and look at the boxes on the shelves and decide which one to choose.

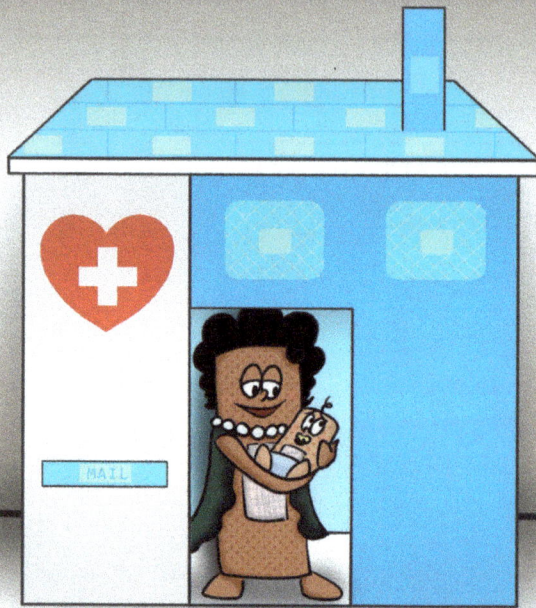

One day, Baby Bandage noticed that a lot of his relatives were moving out. Their shelf was getting empty. He wanted to know where everyone was going and wished that someone would choose his family soon. He asked his mom when somebody would be coming to take his family home, and she said, "I know waiting is hard, but it will happen. We have to be *patient* and our turn will come."

Every morning when the store opened, Baby heard a lot of noise and knew that people would be walking past his shelf. He secretly kept wishing, "Pick me! Pick me!" And then, one exciting day, it happened! A woman with a nice smile grabbed his tiny cardboard home and placed it in her shopping cart. His family got tossed around while the cart rolled down the aisles, but that was okay. They were off to a new adventure!

When the woman got home, she unpacked her bag and found a nice spot in the medicine cabinet for the Bandage family. They had only been living there for a few hours when, all of a sudden, the roof of their tiny home flew open, and Papa was pulled out in a hurry. "Well guys, I'm off. Someone got hurt on the job. Love you. See ya!" he said, as he kissed the family goodbye.

The next day, Bella was called after someone needed to get a shot, leaving just Mama, Bobby and Baby Bandage at home. Baby kept secretly wishing, "Pick me! Pick me!" but nobody seemed to want a tiny baby sized stick-on bandage.

Bobby was picked next. He was just the right size for a middle-size cut. It sure was getting quiet in the cardboard box. Now, just Mama and Baby were left at home. Baby Bandage didn't know why nobody wanted him to do the job. He kept thinking, "I'm just a kid. They don't think I can help." But he knew he could, if he was given a chance.

Uh oh… Mama was needed on the soccer field for a scraped knee. She hugged and kissed Baby before she left and said, "I love you. You are special and so important. Someone will figure that out and will be so happy to get you."

Baby waited and waited in his tiny cardboard box. It felt lonely and empty, and he was getting bored, but he knew he would be okay until someone picked him up. A long, long time went by before he suddenly heard crying. It was coming from a small child, and a woman's kind voice showed that she was trying to help the child feel better. They went into the bathroom where she washed the cut, kissed the child and said, "I have just the right thing."

The woman carefully took Baby Bandage out of the box and said, "I have the perfect tiny bandage for your booboo." She took the thin paper cover off Baby Bandage and, ever so gently, wrapped Baby around the child's small finger. It was exactly THE RIGHT SIZE. Baby Bandage felt so excited to be like a shield and protect a booboo. His turn had come. He felt useful and proud to help, and the child smiled.

The shelf in the store began to fill up with new relatives. Some moved in, and some moved out. But Baby Bandage had a new home. He was now living on a little finger that ate messy food and played with toys and paint and sand and slime and played sports. He sat on one little finger of a small hand that didn't like to use soap very much. Baby finally had a job to do. Even though he was little, Baby Bandage felt very important. He knew he could help and he did.

22

# Glossary

**Adhesive tape**:    A long strip of tape used to stick things together, especially for medical purposes.

**Alcohol**: A chemical liquid that kills germs and prevents infection outside of the body.

**Antiseptic**: A chemical substance that stops or slows germs from growing.

**Blister**: A raised place on the skin that has a watery liquid inside.

**Elastic bandage**: A stretchy fabric used to wrap around part of the body that hurts from a muscle sprain or strain.

**First aid**: Fast action taken to help a person who has been hurt or is having a medical emergency.

**Gauze**: A thin, white, woven, fabric bandage that can absorb wet things.

**Ice pack**: Cold gel or frozen water that is used to help sprains and bruises or swollen parts of the body.

**Injury**: the part of your body that is hurt from physical harm or damage.

**Wound**: An opening in the skin caused by a scrape, puncture, blister or cut.

**Scab**: A hard covering, formed by special blood cells from your body, that protects a wound from dirt and germs.

# Parent and Caregiver Guide

Fact: children grow. Their small bodies and minds are programmed to develop throughout their lives. As they progress through various stages of development, propelled by curiosity about the world around them, they are active in their pursuits of skill, fun, stimulation and knowledge. Since experimentation and practice lead to mastery, children engage in hours upon hours of activities throughout the course of their busy day. A child's work is never done.

However, with that innocent lust for life comes some risk. Small cuts, scraped knees, sports injuries, trips and falls and lacerations are common and expected. Bigger things, such as illness, surgeries, accidents or emergencies, sometimes occur, as well. All of these issues may require some form of first aid or medical intervention. In a way that is amusing, informative, developmentally appropriate and anxiety free, this book is intended to provide the most basic understanding of medical applications that a child might encounter following an injury. It can also provide a launching platform for parents who wish to delve into more serious conversations or explanations specific to their child.

In the event that your child needs some form of care, it is important for you to remain as calm as possible, as children take their cues from the adults they trust. Speak softly and move slowly as you explain to your child what is needed. Since bruises and cuts are inevitable in childhood, it is wise to keep all your first aid supplies together to avoid a frantic search for the things you need if an emergency were to arise. You may also want to keep important phone numbers of doctors and urgent care centers in the same place.

Science has taught us that anxiety increases one's perception of pain. It is also true that when people feel prepared, they feel more control over a situation. Therefore, reading *Baby Bandage and His First Aid Family: Healing Little Hurts and Booboos* to your child now, as you might any other story, will help them feel best prepared when the day comes that they need care. It is my sincere hope your family and you enjoy this book, and that it helps your child feel reassured by having the information before they actually need it.

# About the Author

**Dr. Laurie Zelinger's** passion for helping children is reflected in her work and numerous books that tackle issues of concern to children and their families. She is a board-certified psychologist and credentialed play therapist with over 45 years' experience working in schools, developmental centers and private agencies, as well as in her busy private practice, devoted exclusively to children. Her passion for writing began when she discovered journaling in third grade, and which was then fortified in fourth grade when she wrote a play that was performed by students in her public school. As an adult, she has successfully blended her love of helping children with her writing talent, creating topical, educational books that appeal to kids and their parents.

Dr. Zelinger's books for Loving Healing Press include: *Please Explain Anxiety to Me: Simple Biology and Solutions for Children and Parents, Please Explain "Time Out" to Me: A Story for Children and Do-It-Yourself Manual for Parents, Please Explain Vaccines to Me Because I Hate Shots!", Please Explain Alzheimer's Disease to Me: A Children's Story and Parent Handbook About Dementia", Please Explain Tonsillectomy & Adenoidectomy to Me: A Complete Guide to Preparing Your Child for Surgery* and *Please Explain Terrorism to Me: A Story for Children and P-E-A-R-L-S of Wisdom for Their Parents!* Dr. Zelinger has also worked with American Girl where she wrote *A Smart Girl's Guide to Liking Herself Even On The Bad Days* and is credited with being a consultant for their Bitty Baby book series, where she assisted in the development of the "For Parents" sections. In addition, Dr. Zelinger has written for *Play Therapy* magazine, as well as for therapeutic books, where her chapters offer strategies that can be used with fearful children.

Dr. Zelinger's additional credentials include media referral specialist for the American Psychological Association, four years as director on the executive board of the New York Association of Play Therapy and an elected position as officer in the American Academy of School Psychology. As a sought-after expert on children's behavior, Dr. Zelinger has contributed to nearly 200 venues regarding child development. She and her psychologist husband, Dr. Fred, are both certified Red Cross Disaster Mental Health volunteers. They have been happily married for over 40 years, have raised four children and relish their roles as grandparents.

www.ingramcontent.com/pod-product-compliance
Lightning Source LLC
Chambersburg PA
CBHW061407090426
42739CB00022B/3500